THE ABSOLUTE ESSENTIAL
ZOMBIE
COLORING BOOK

BRENT METCALF + RYAN J. RHOADES

The Absolute Essential Zombie Coloring Book

© Copyright 2017, Brent Metcalf & Ryan J. Rhoades

All artwork © 2017, Brent Metcalf & Ryan J. Rhoades. All rights reserved.

No part of this book may be reproduced in any manner without the express written permission of the authors, in advance. **You can connect with the authors at bipster.net & reformationdesigns.com**

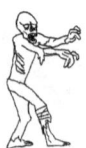

Scratch Page

A place for you to test your colors and claw marks before engraving them indelibly on the final works of art.

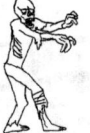

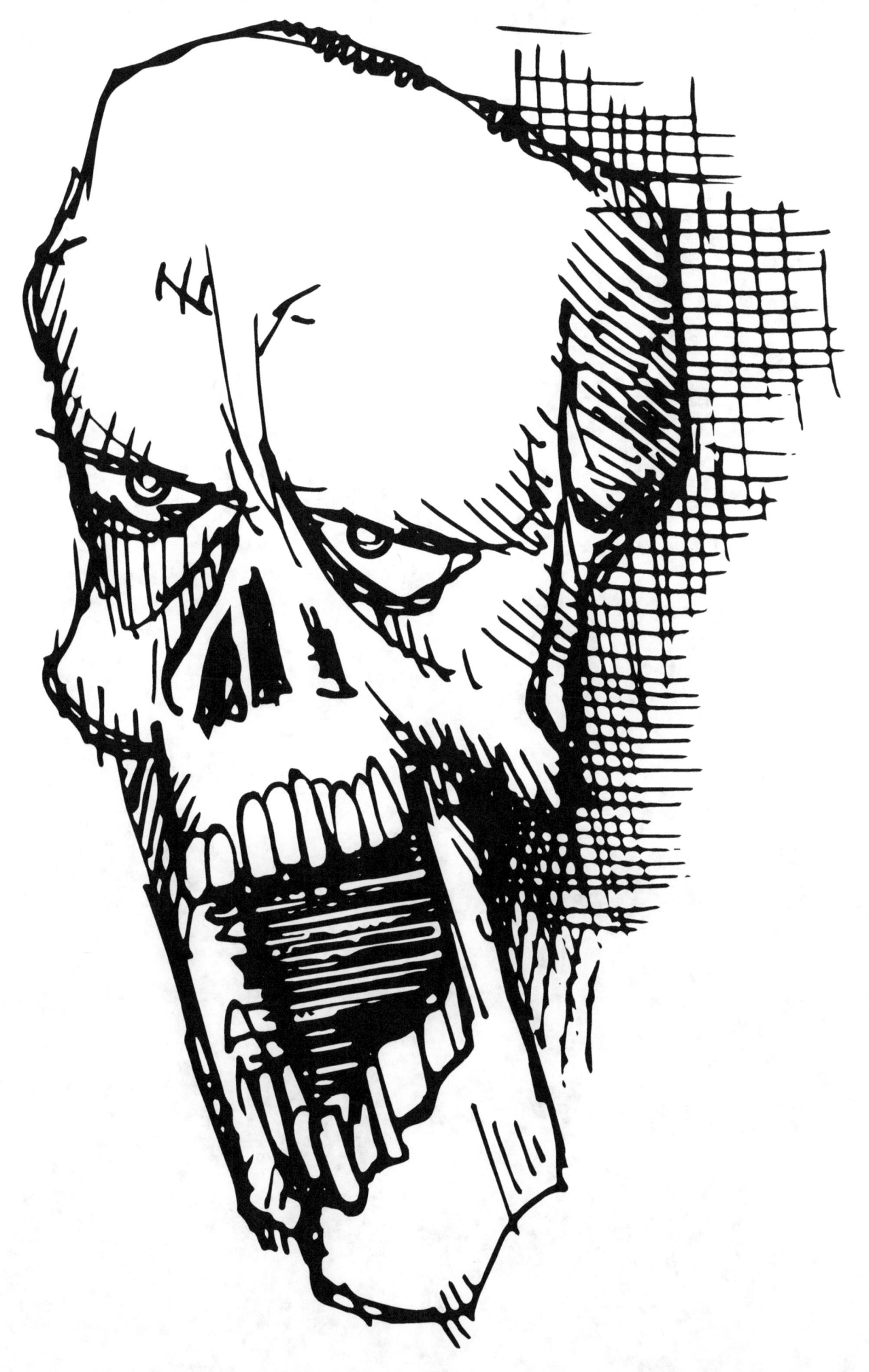

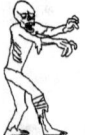

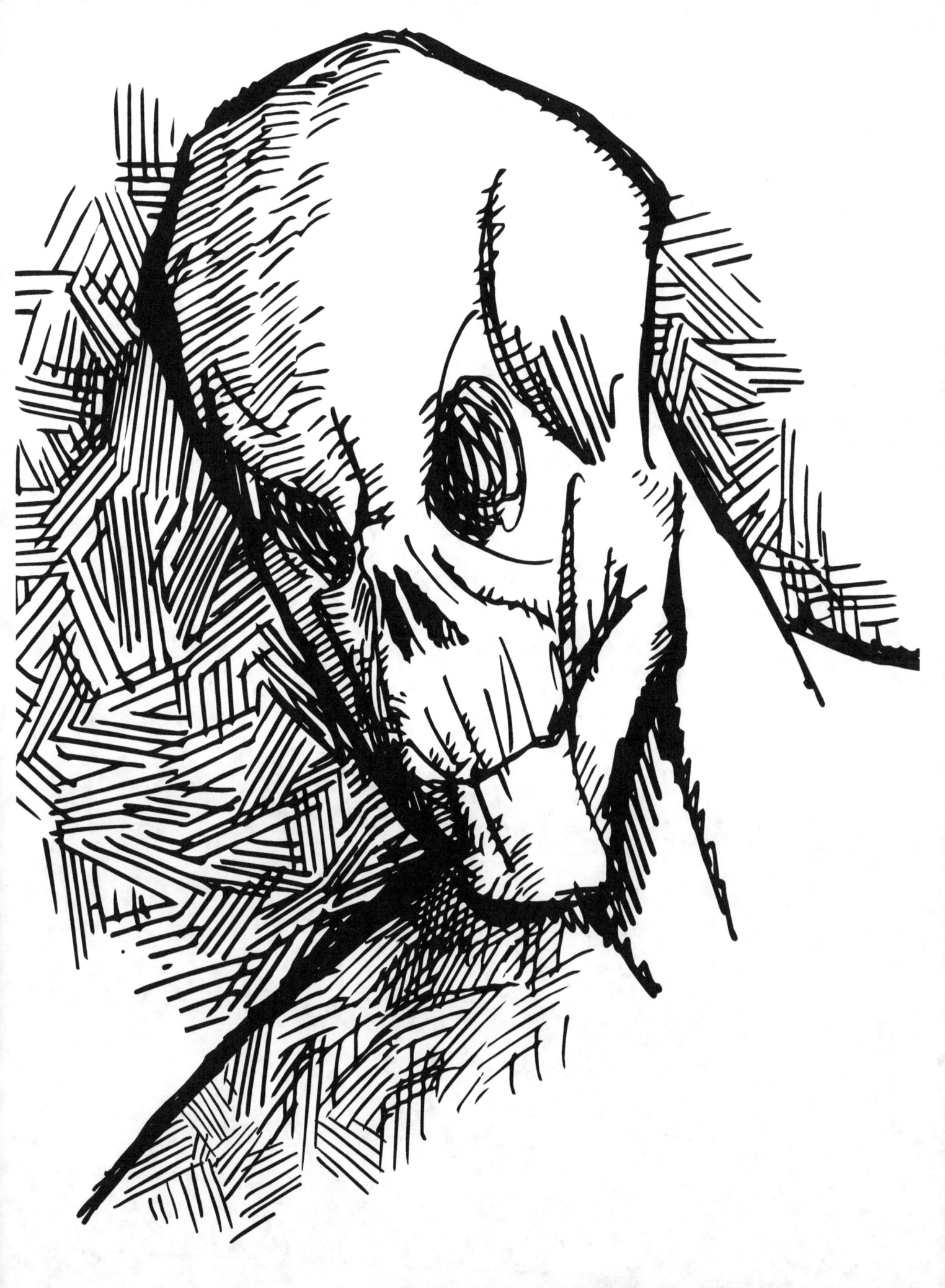

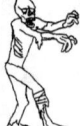

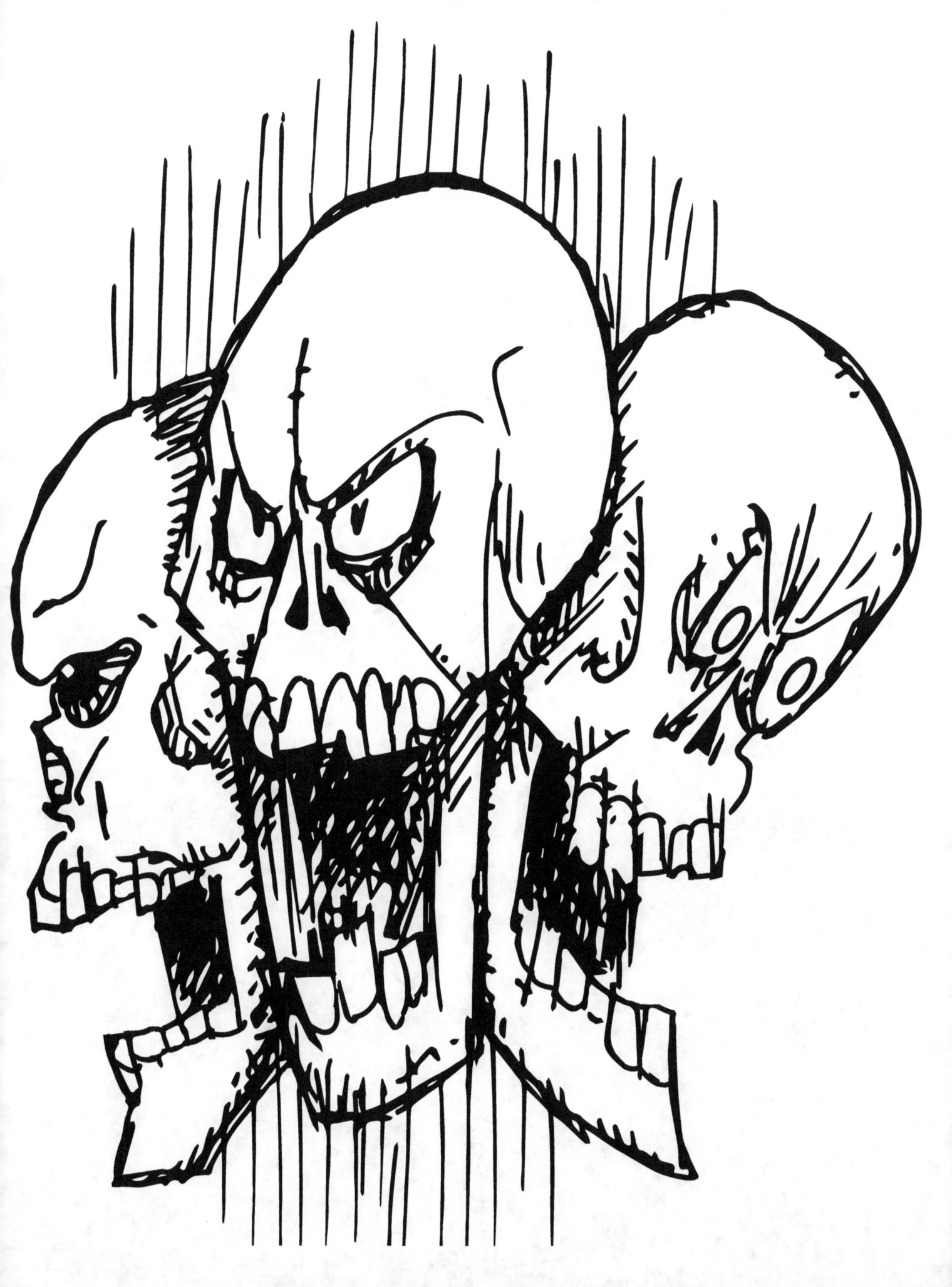

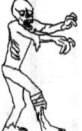

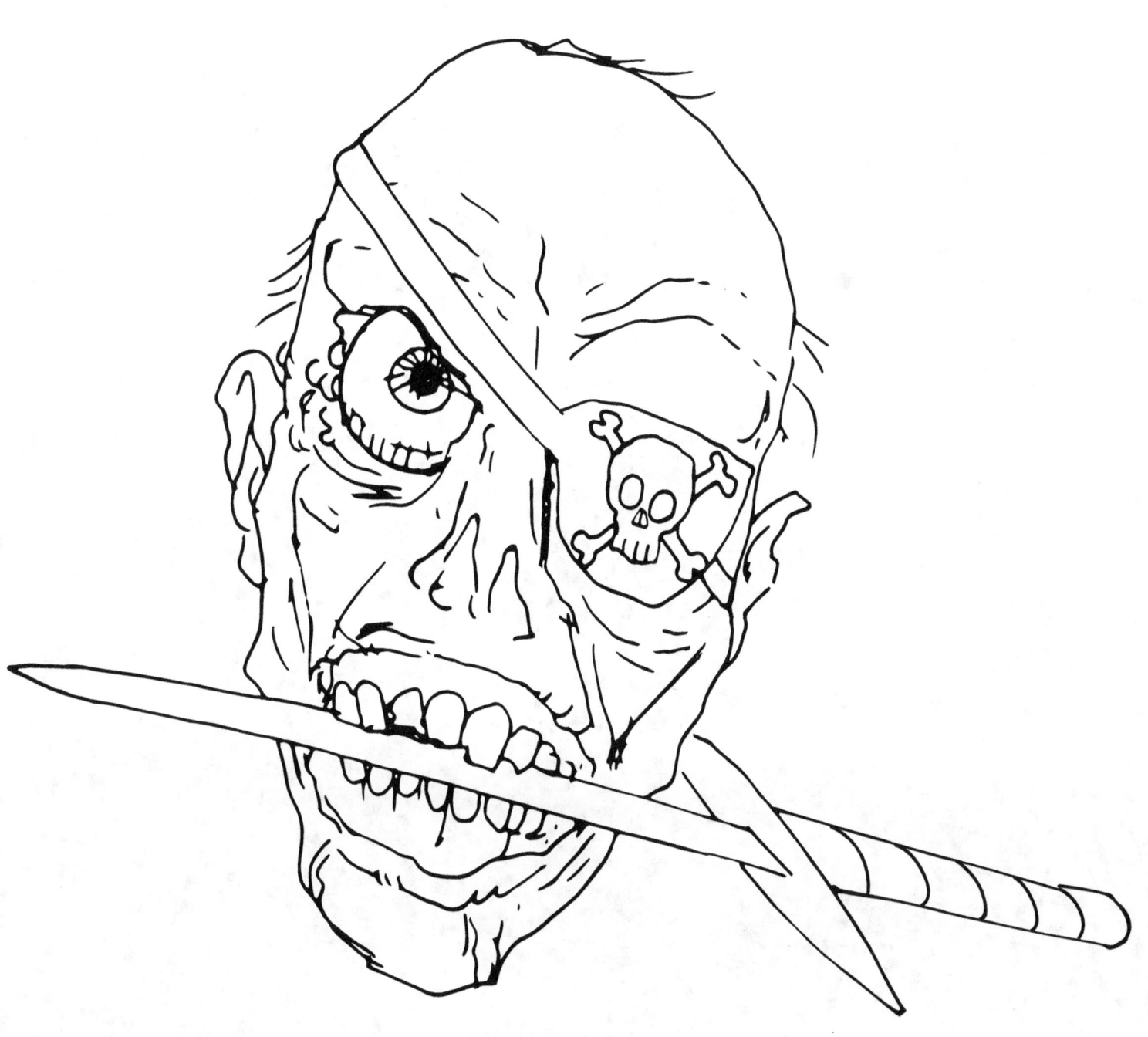

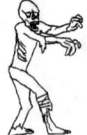

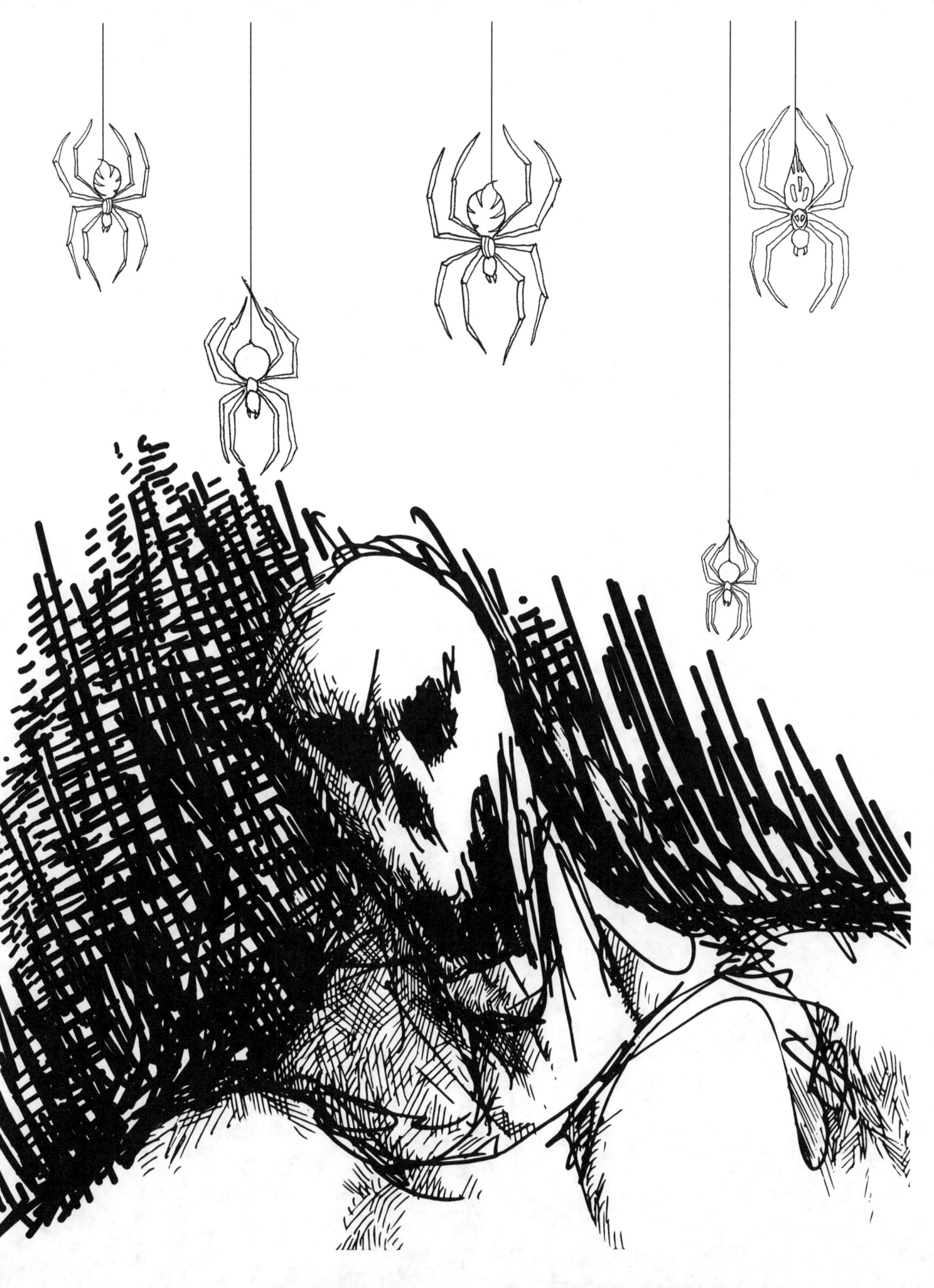

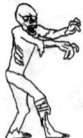

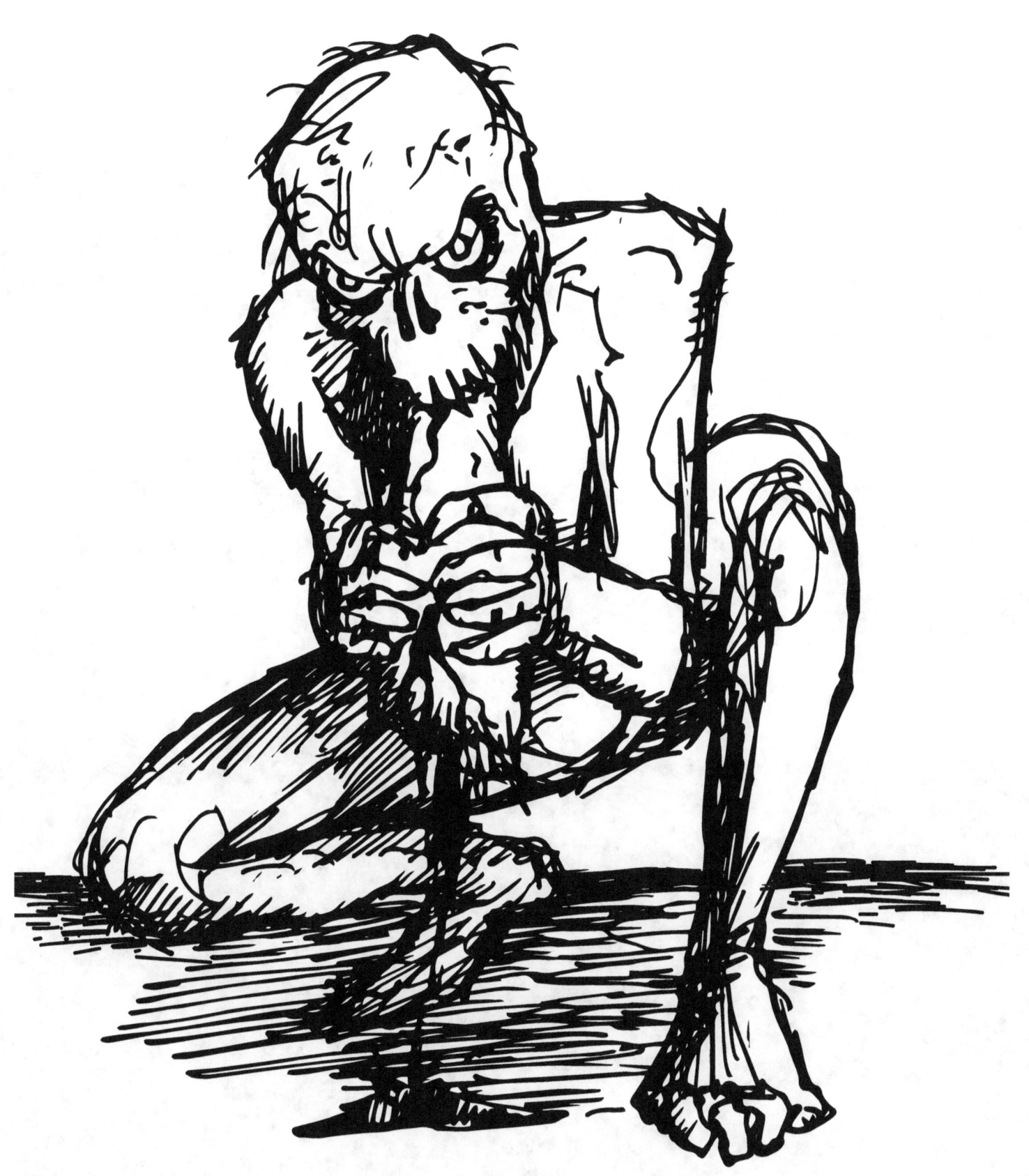

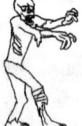

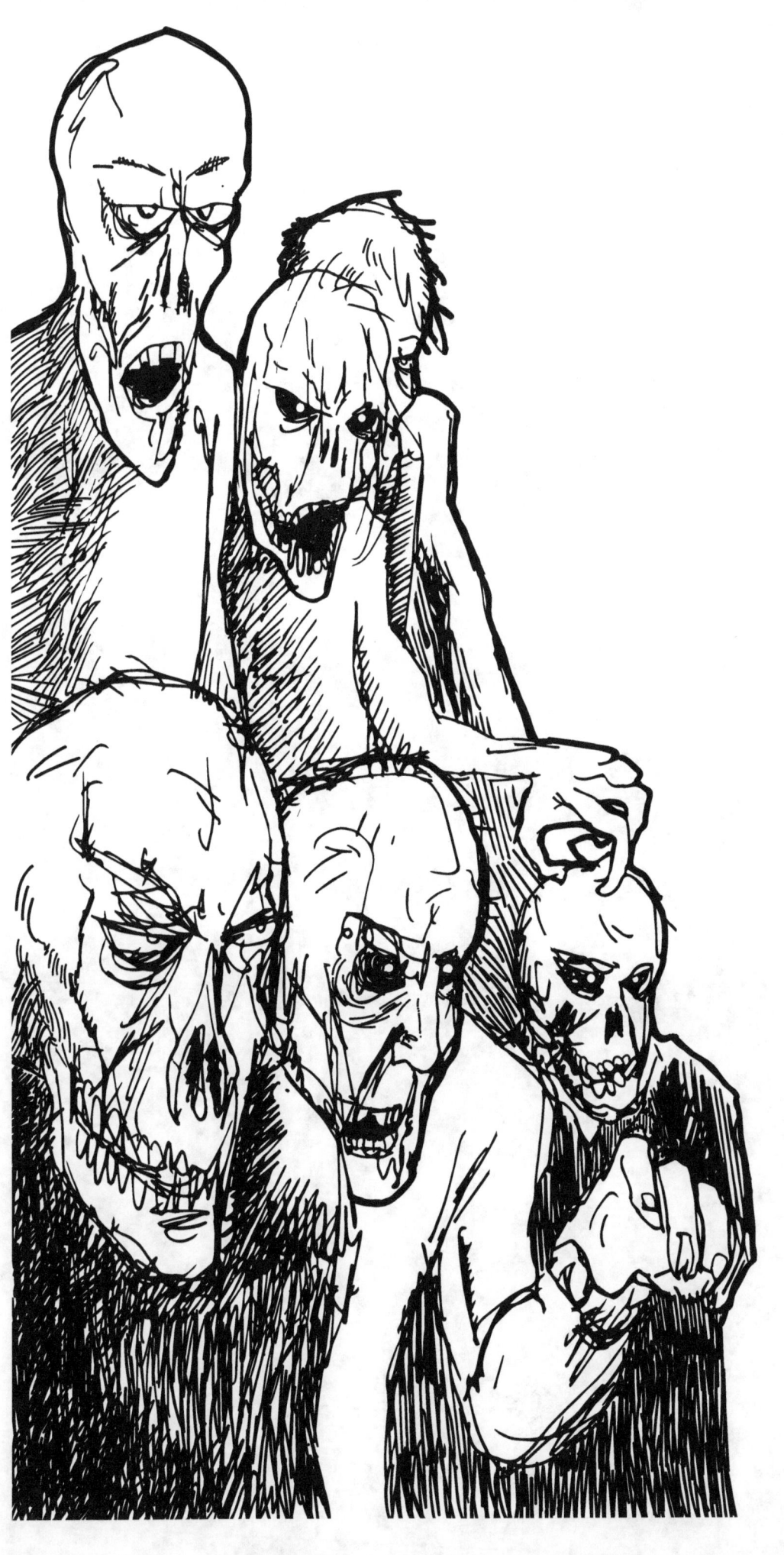

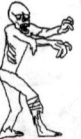

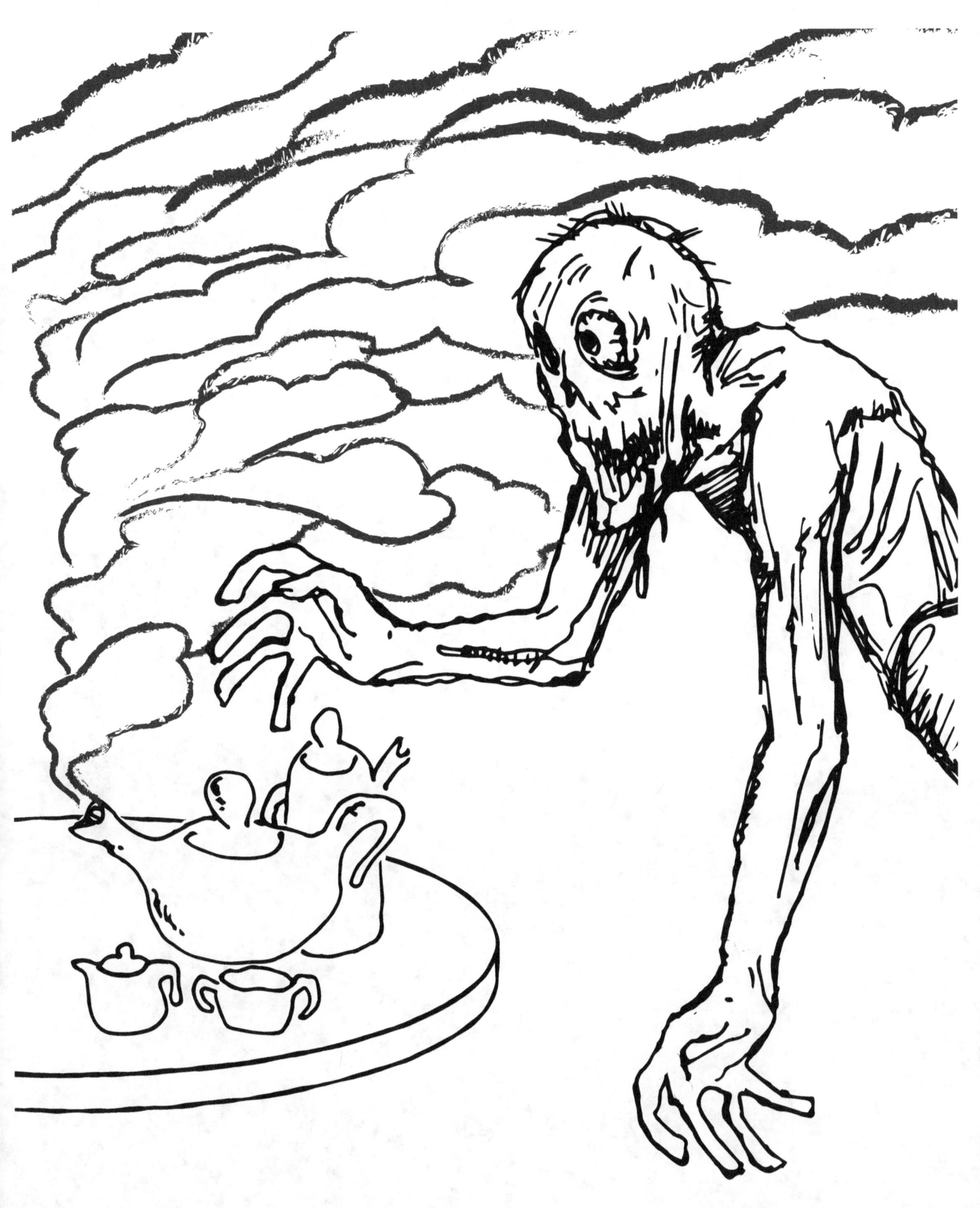

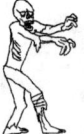

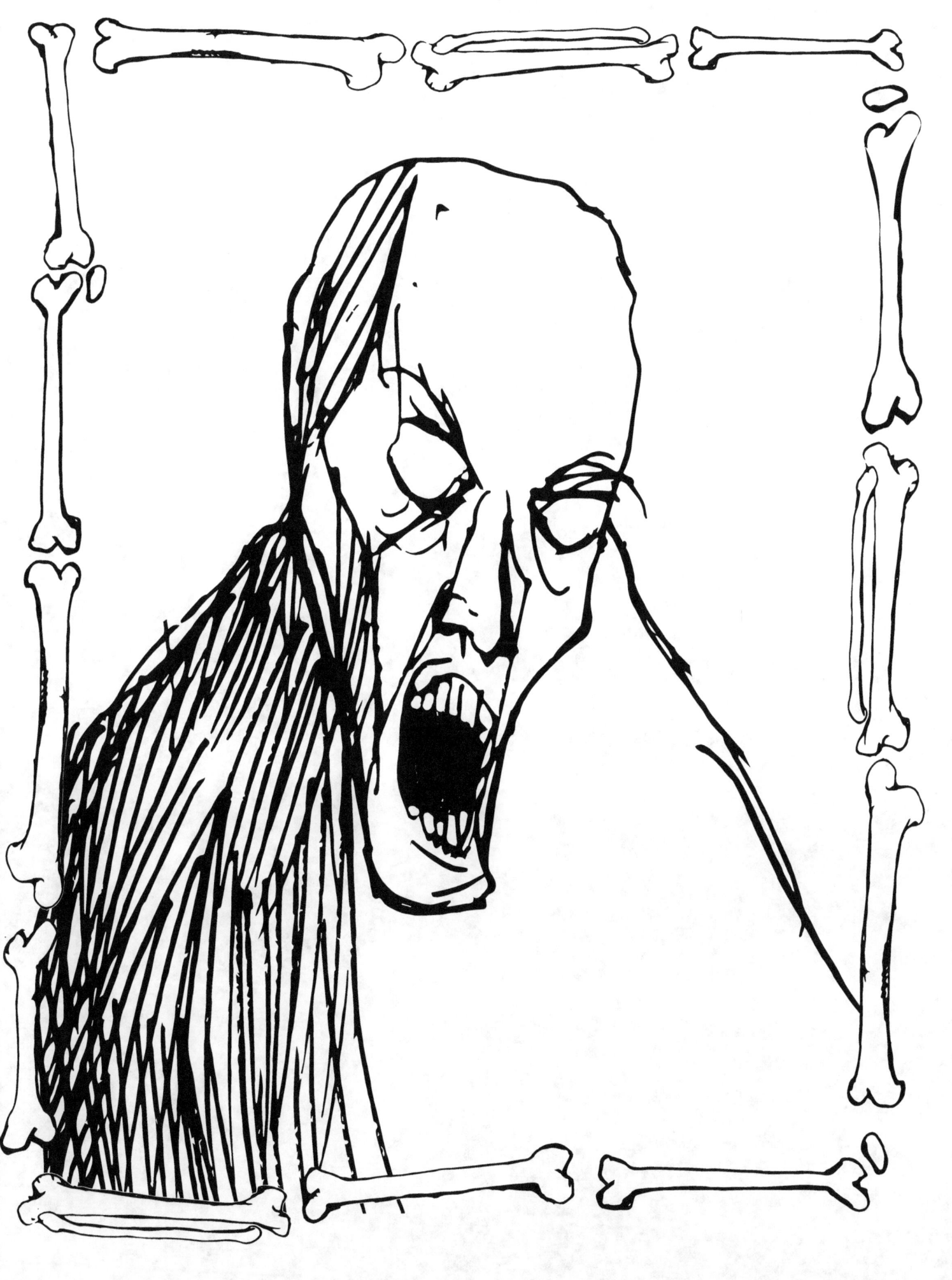

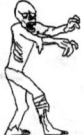

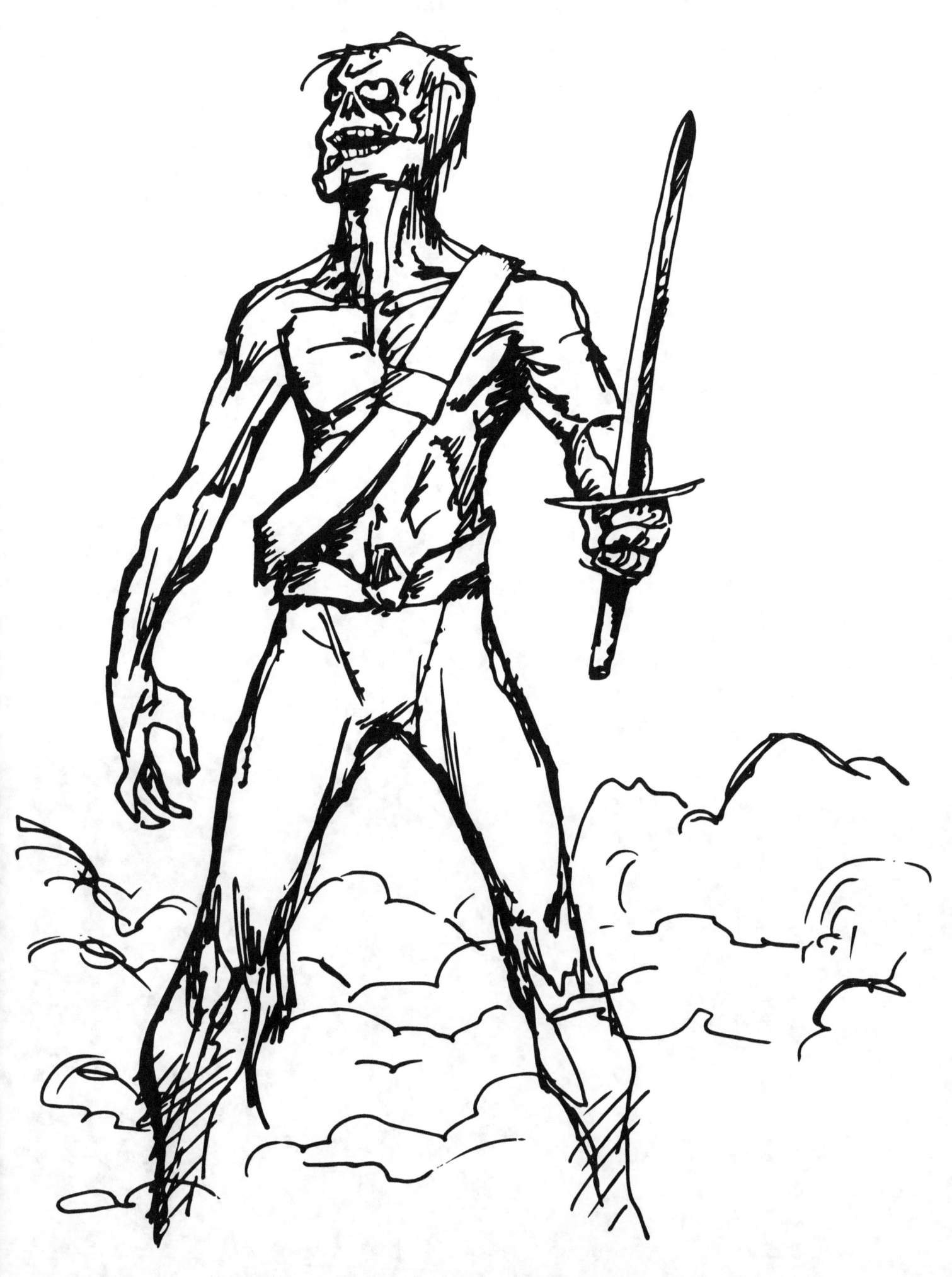

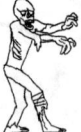

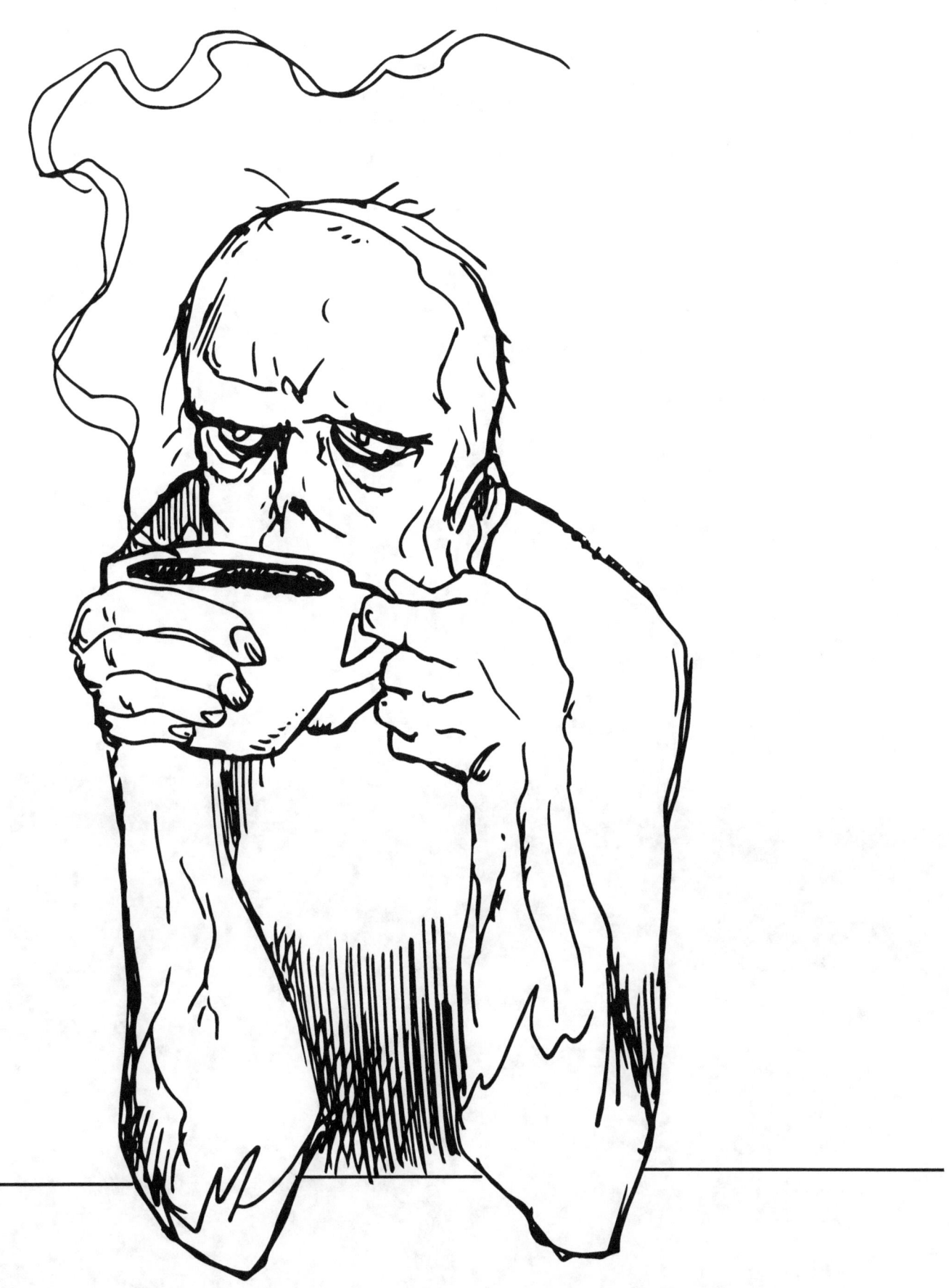

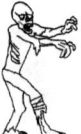

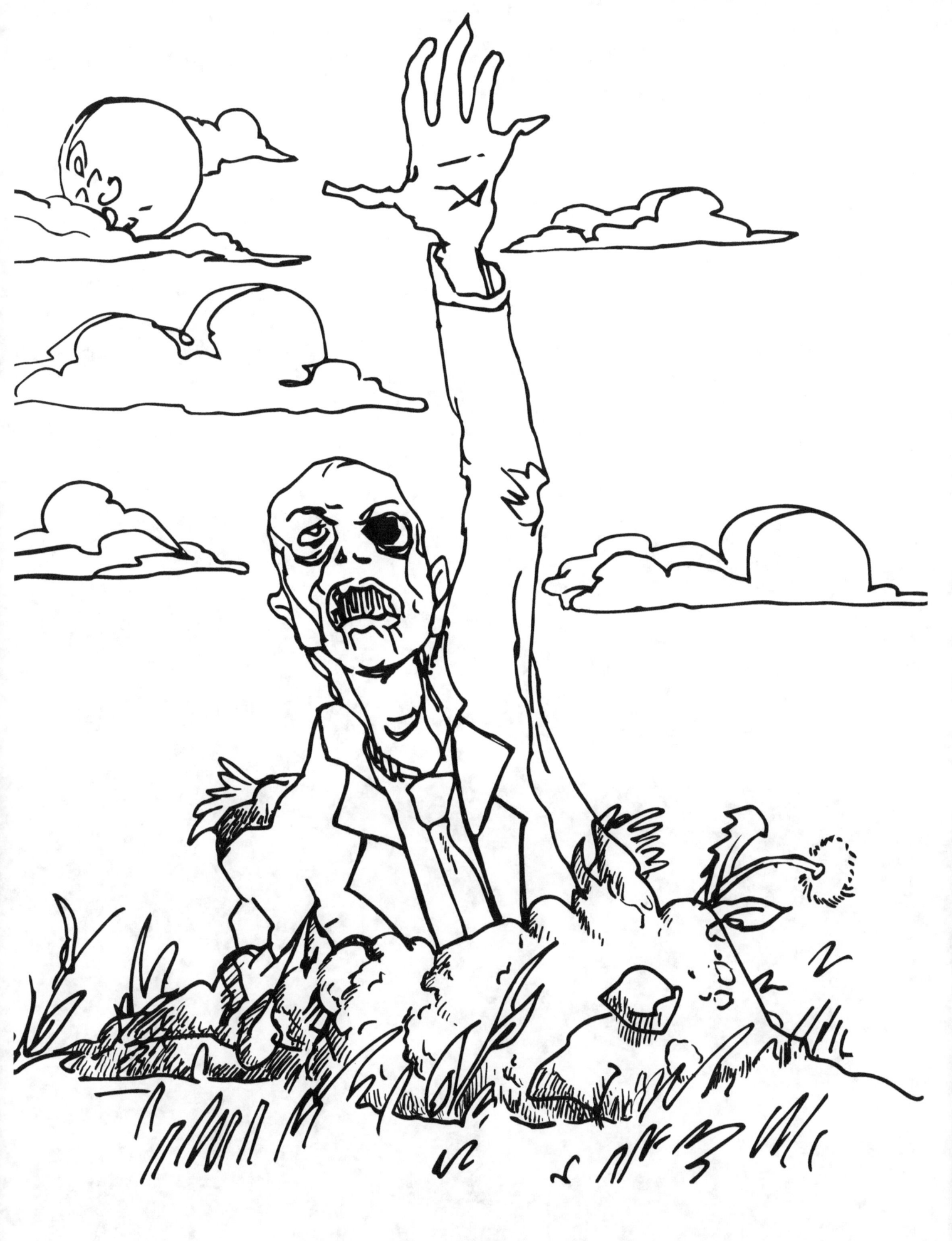

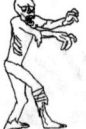

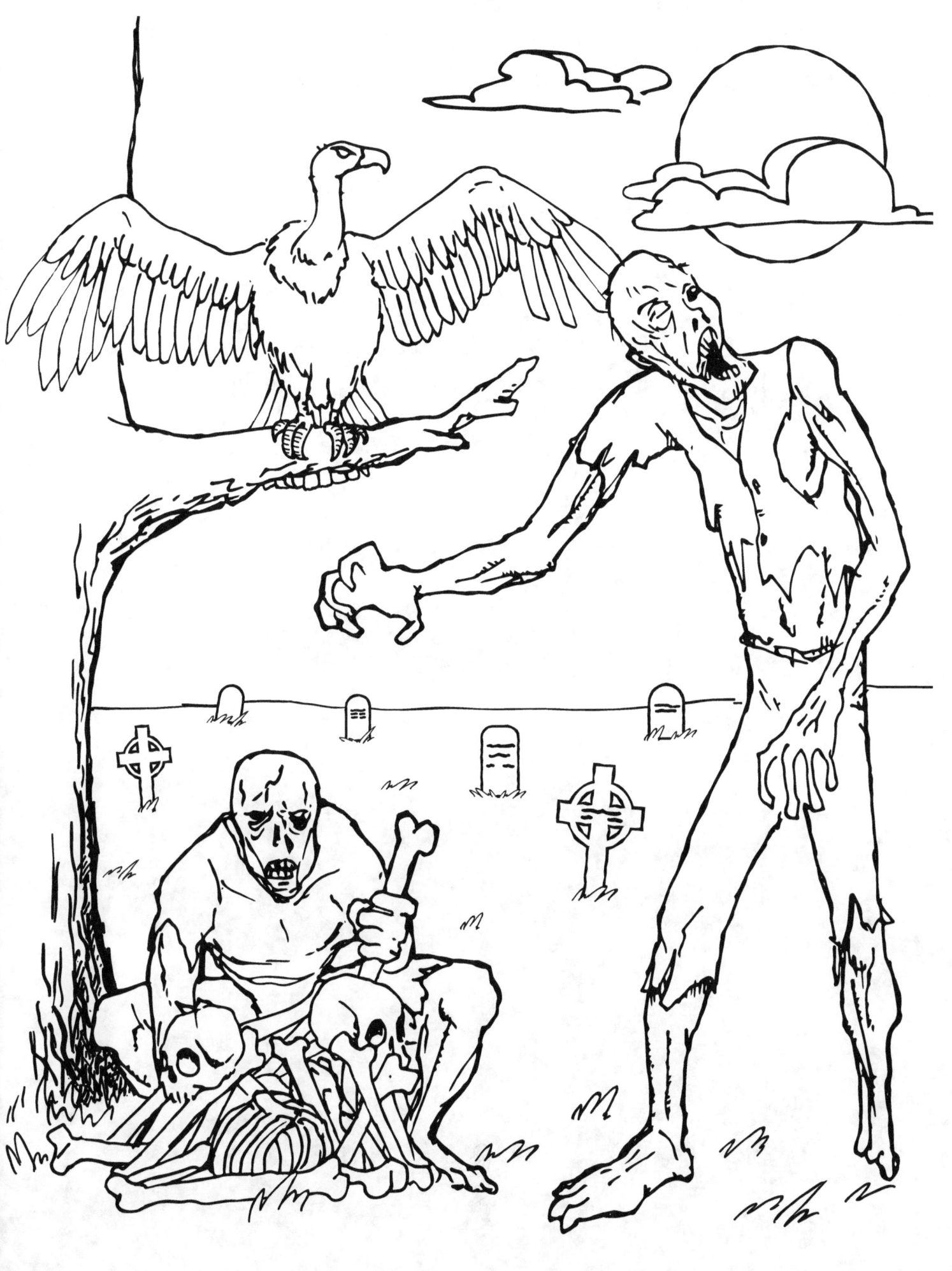

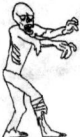

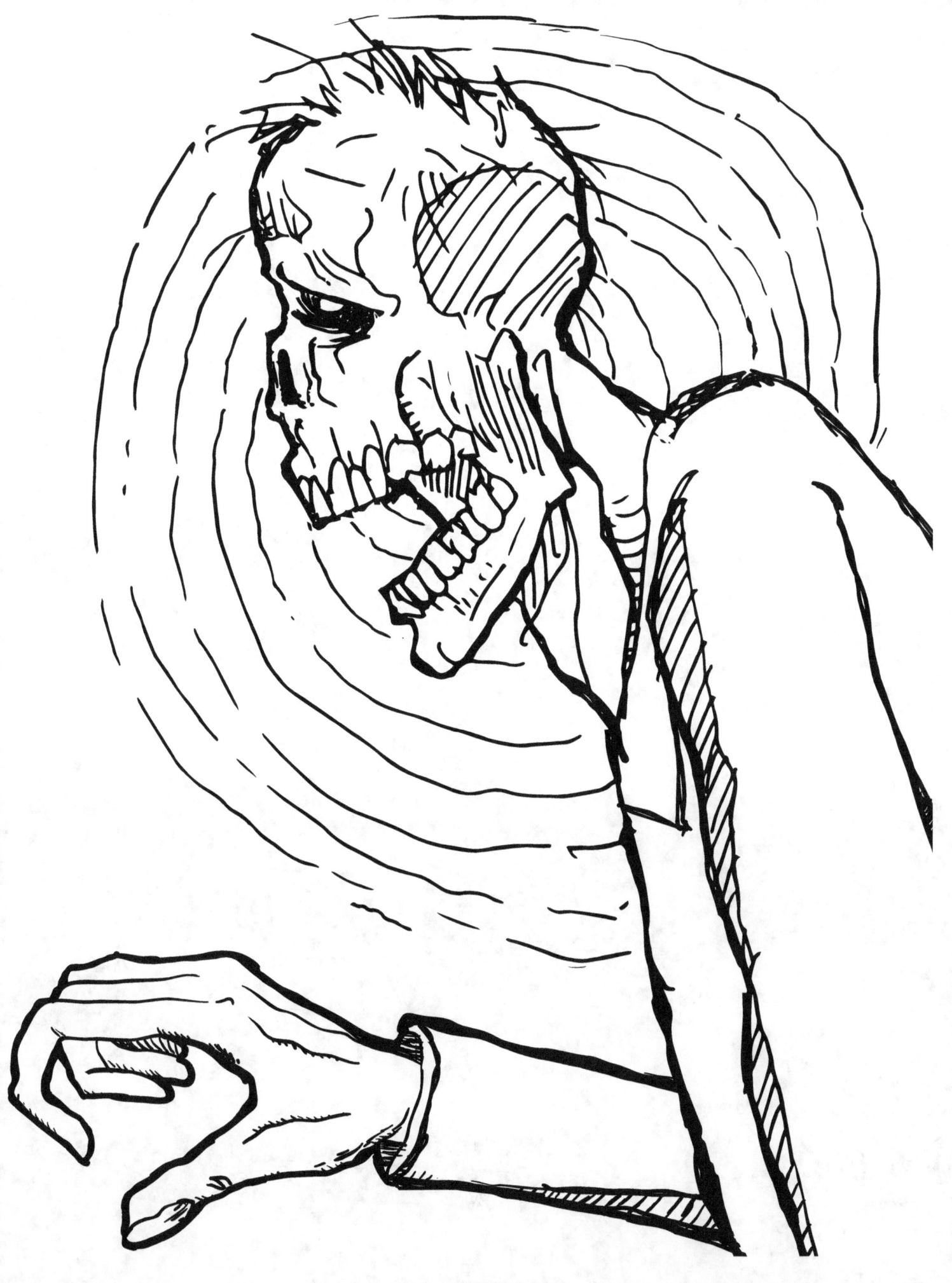

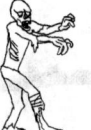

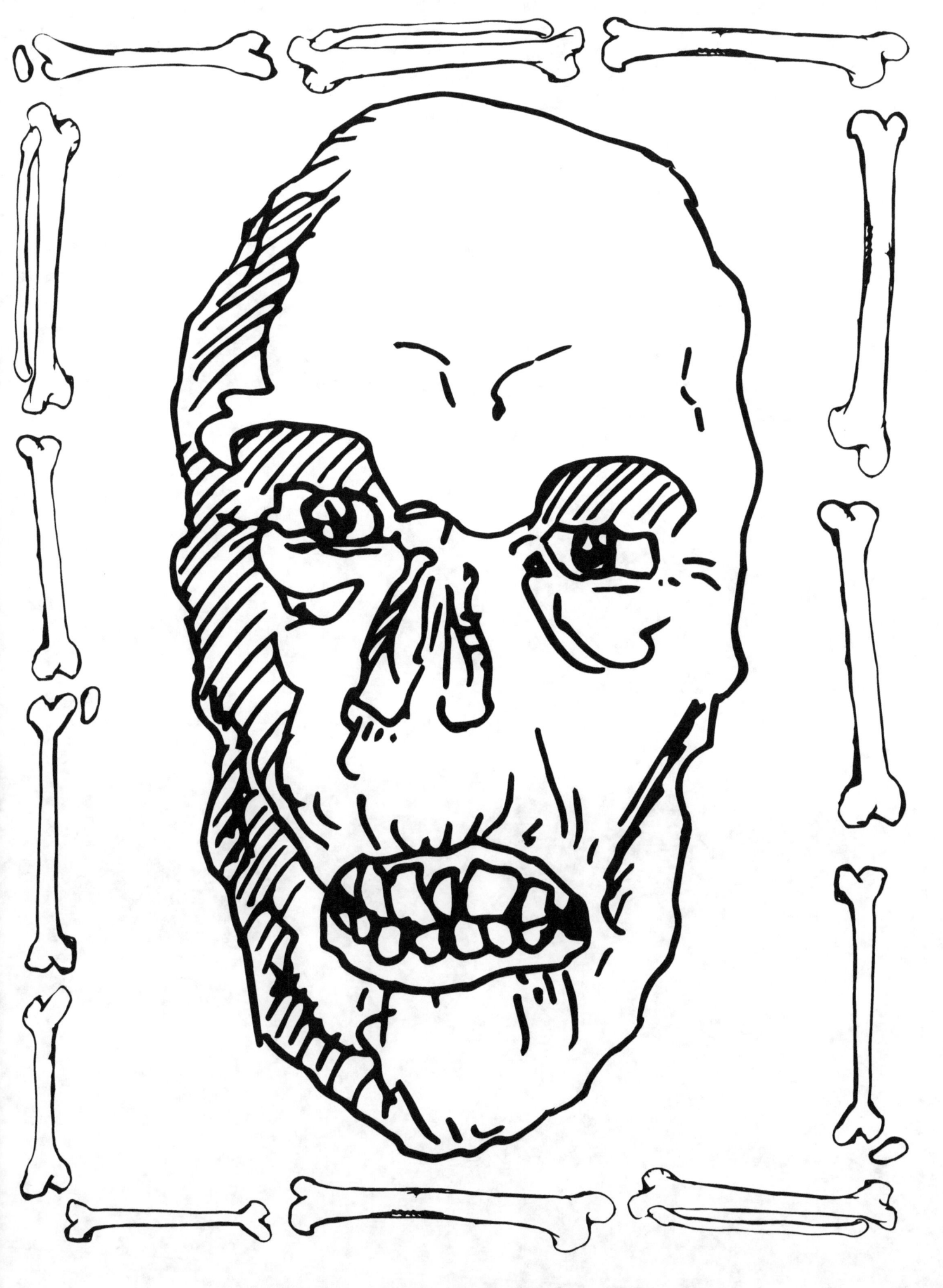

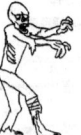

34

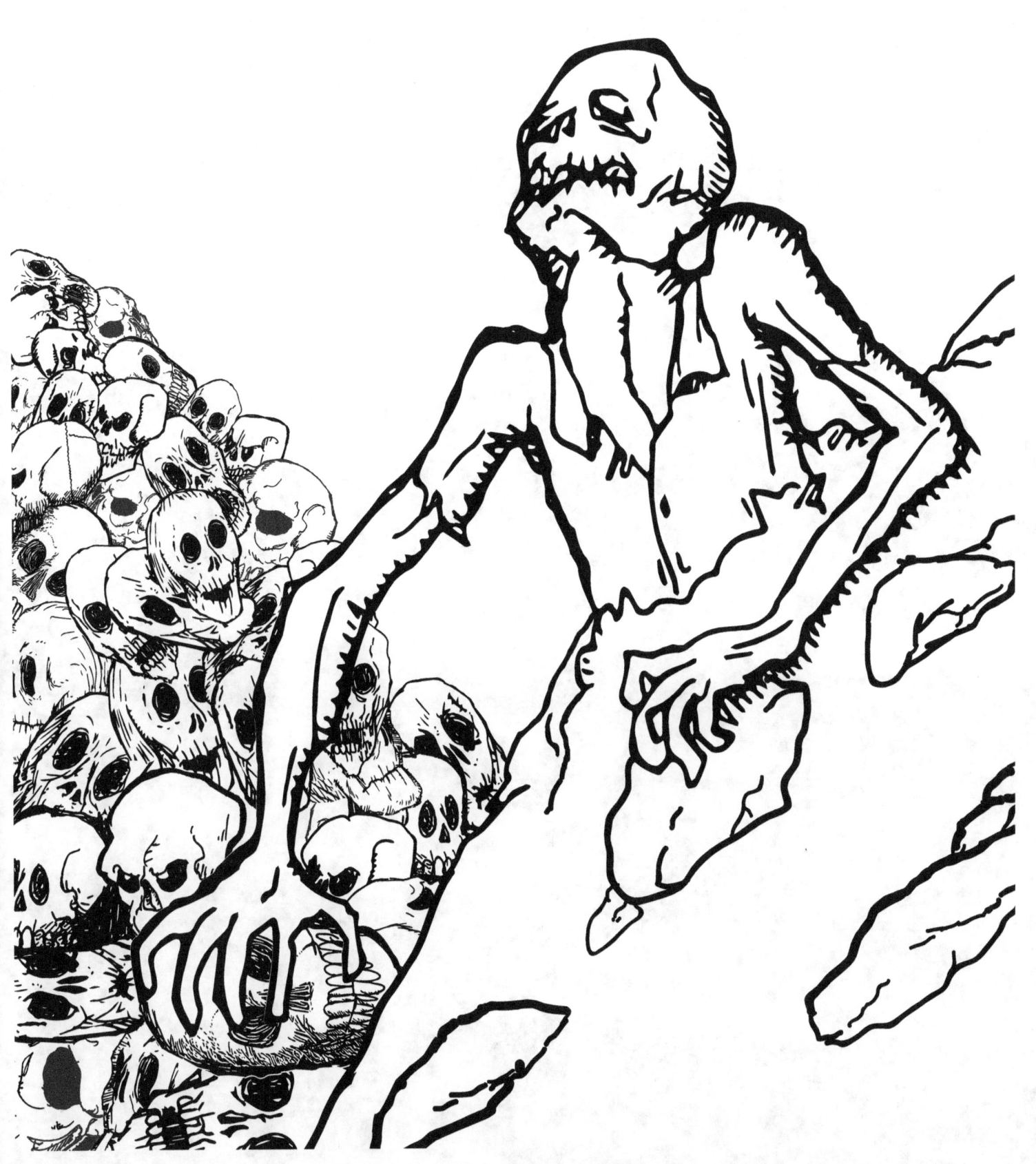

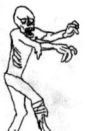

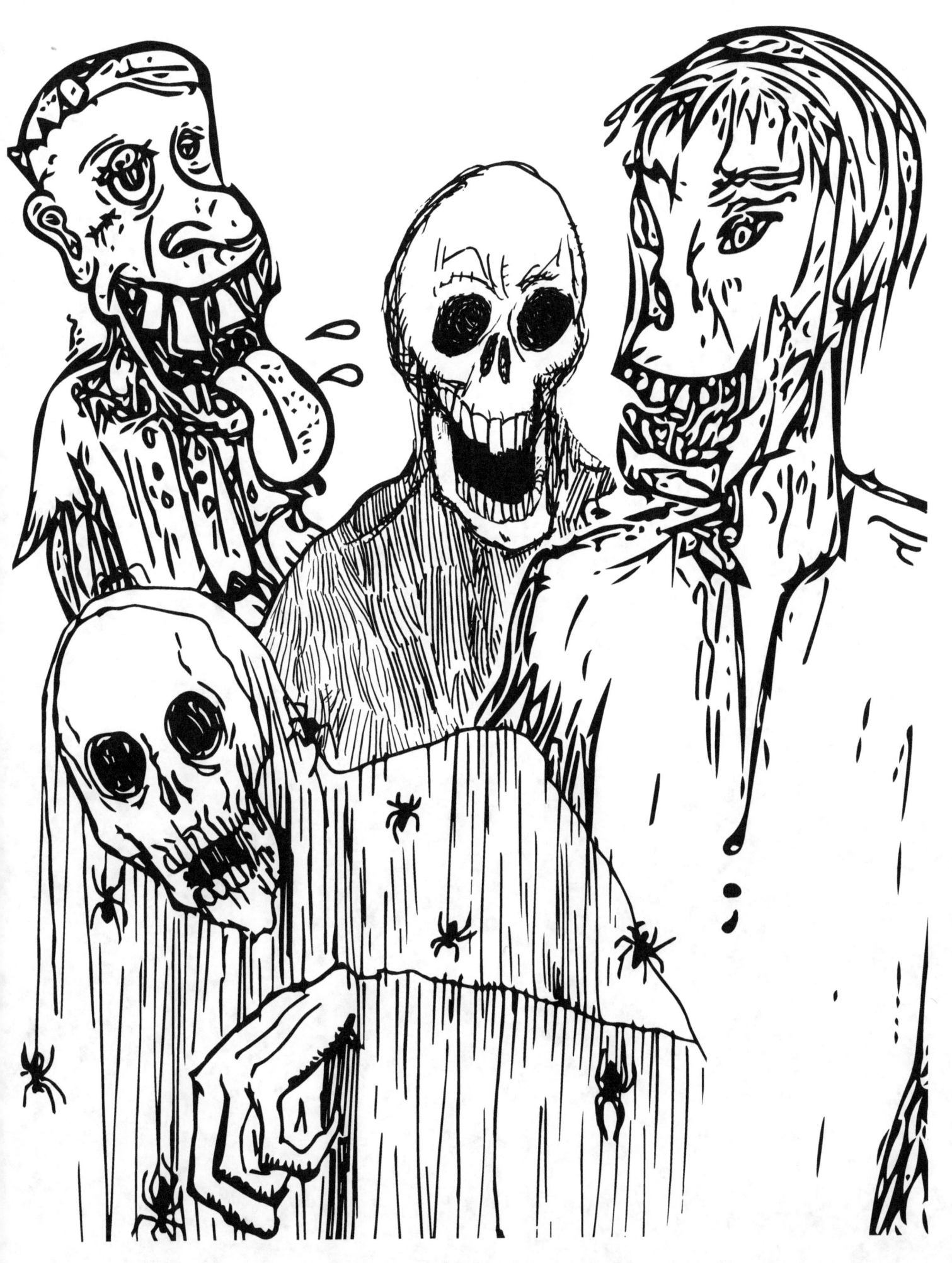

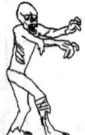

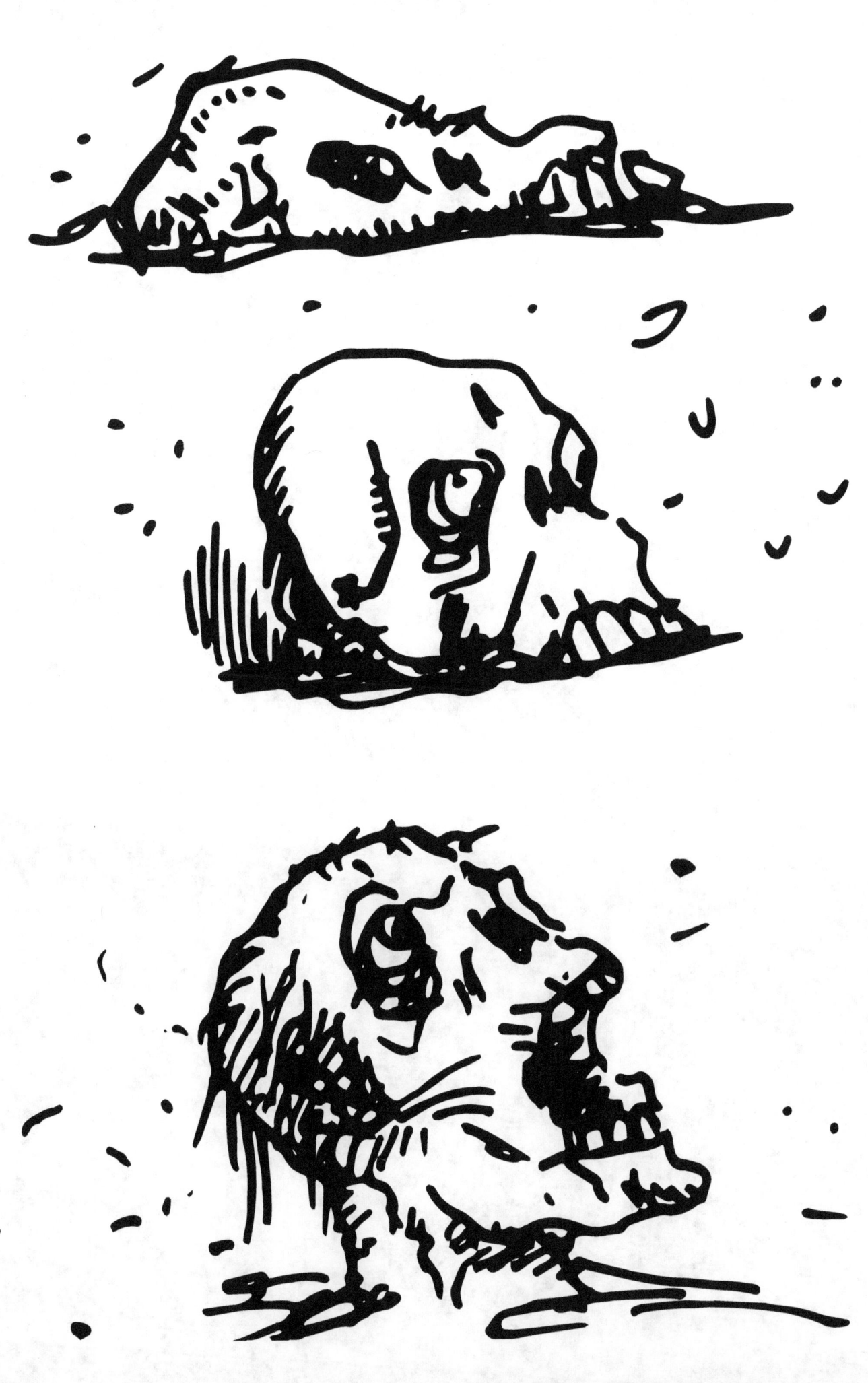

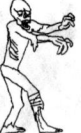

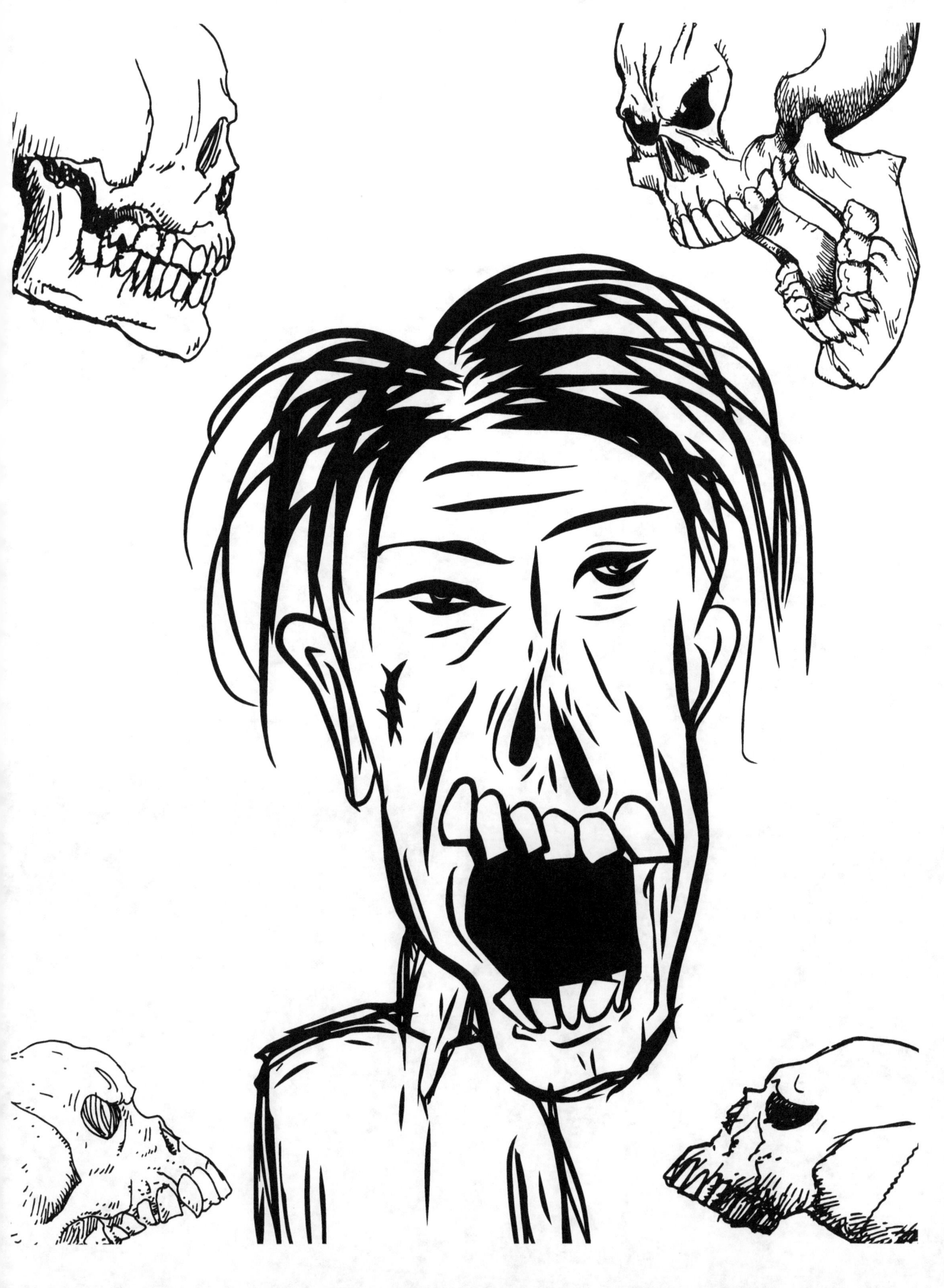

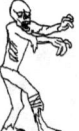

DID YOU ENJOY THIS COLORING BOOK?

PLEASE LEAVE US A REVIEW ON AMAZON AND LET US KNOW!

SHARE YOUR CREATIONS WITH US BY CONTACTING US AT BIPSTER.NET + REFORMDESIGNS.BIZ

FOLLOW US ON INSTAGRAM: @BIPORAMA & @REFORMDESIGNS

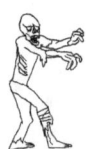

www.ingramcontent.com/pod-product-compliance
Lightning Source LLC
Chambersburg PA
CBHW081309180526
45170CB00007B/2630